D0725516

STETSON MANSION

Love and kindness are the greatest of gifts. Give them often.

J Thompson

STETSON MANSION

How to Polish a Diamond
A Journey of Restoration and Self Discovery

JT Thompson

RICK SCOTT
GOVERNOR

August 18, 2014

Dear Friends:

Congratulations on the Stetson Mansion's success and being named Florida's most-liked tourist attraction by TripAdvisor. You are to be commended for your dedication and commitment to preserving one of Florida's historic treasures.

Thank you for offering residents and visitors opportunities to enjoy Florida's rich history. As you help attract visitors to our state, you are helping to strengthen our state's economy. Increased tourism allows businesses to succeed and provides more jobs for Floridians, which is why my goal is to attract 100 million tourists to our state in 2014. Thank you for your efforts to help us reach that goal.

Again, congratulations, and you have my best wishes for your continued success.

Sincerely,

Rick Scott
Governor

This shadow of a cowboy is cast on the wall of the staircase when the chandelier is on. A friend discovered it as she was leaving the Gillen Suite one day and snapped this picture. I think this is so incredibly cool, it's as if Mr. Stetson is watching over the mansion.

Contents

DEDICATION

I dedicate this book to all those who attack each day armed with their imaginations and beliefs of what could be and not necessarily what is. For you the parameters of reality are just lines drawn in the sand continually being expanded and redrawn. So for all you dreamers out there – this one's for you.

FOREWORD

> *"What this power is I cannot say; all I know is that it exists and it becomes available only when a man is in that state of mind in which he knows exactly what he wants and is fully determined not to quit until he finds it."*
>
> *-Alexander Graham Bell*

The belief that success originates from trained thought has been expressed by many of the most influential people this world has come to know, including William Shakespeare, Ralph Waldo Emerson, Thomas Alva Edison, Albert Einstein, and Henry Ford, to name merely a few. However, as Alexander Graham Bell stated, the secret to unlocking this power and accomplishing incredible feats lies in commitment and unwavering perseverance. Hence, many are able to dream, but few have the courage to act upon those dreams.

I was leading a seminar with first-year students on the power of positive thinking when the courageous JT Thompson entered my life. Networked through a mutual friend that recognized my shared beliefs on the strength of dominant thoughts, JT offered to provide my class with a guided tour of the Stetson Mansion. During this personal tour, I came to know the magnificence of JT and of the mansion he and Michael Solari presently call "home."

In 2005, when JT and Michael first visited the Stetson Mansion, it had been lived in for nearly 30 years. Yet upon the very first steps inside, the home seemingly came alive. By virtue of its impressive character, it was as if John B. Stetson himself was providing JT and Michael with a tour of his home that was the largest, grandest most historical home built before the 20th century in the state of Florida. JT was mesmerized by the intricate parquet flooring constructed in three dimensional designs, the hand-crafted stained glass windows colored in a Tiffany-like fashion, and the original Edison circuit box adorned with tags hand-written by its installer, Mr. Thomas A. Edison himself. In that instant, JT saw the Mansion for what it was: a historical treasure buried under years of neglect, dust and disrepair, waiting for someone to tell its story of birth and rebirth.

Upon purchasing the Mansion, JT and Michael had no idea how they would obtain the enormous amount of funds necessary to restore the mansion's grandeur. In fact, it would have been easiest to agree with the scores of others who said it was impossible, but neither was willing to constrain their dreams by such pragmatic considerations. JT and Michael simply committed to reaching the finish line without any clue as to what the course would behold.

This book is about the glorious history of the Stetson Mansion, the miraculous occurrences that made the restoration possible, and the personal transformation of the individuals who knew exactly what they wanted and were fully determined not to quit until they found it. Thomas A. Edison once said: "Many of life's failures are people who did not realize how close they were to success when they gave up." JT Thompson and Michael Solari are two guys who dream GIGANTIC and refuse to give up, and because of their unrelenting perseverance they have succeeded in restoring the Stetson Mansion to a grandiose condition and are hence forever woven into its historic fabric.

Maria F. Rickling, Ph.D.
Assistant Professor of Accounting
M.E. Rinker, Sr. Institute of Tax and Accountancy
Stetson University
Deland, Florida

Acknowledgements

Restoring the Stetson Mansion has been a profound journey for me. There are so many people who have helped me pave this road of dreams and I will be eternally grateful for their support and encouragement along the way.

First, to my mom who taught me how to squeeze every drop of living out of life. She reminded me to never succumb to fear and never to live your life for others. Although you are not physically with me anymore, Mom, your presence is always felt. Thank you for teaching me the meaning of unconditional love by your actions, not your words. I miss you.

To Austin, my son. Thank you for giving me the privilege to be your dad. No matter how great my successes, nothing will compare to the joy with which you have filled my heart. As you begin your journey through life as a young man please remember this, try not to become a man of success, but rather try to become a man of value. I love you so much.

To Debbie, Colleen, and Terri, my three sisters, who each in her unique way provided me with an invaluable insight on life without even knowing that they were fueling my dreams. None of us have a choice when it comes to the family cards we are dealt, but I wouldn't trade my hand for all the jackpots in the world.

To the hundreds of showcase sponsors who were willing to believe in my crazy, unorthodox ideas. Because of you, the Stetson Mansion has returned to its original grandeur and found its rightful place back in the spotlight. I realize that I was a huge gamble – especially since I had never taken on a project of this magnitude before. My passion and love for the Mansion drove me; however, so many of you were willing to accept that as reason enough to sign on. You will all be forever embedded in the magic of Stetson Mansion's history and renovation.

And to you, Michael, my best friend, my business partner, my true love, my rock. I thank you most of all. You have always provided me with a safe harbor, a place to which I can always come back for support and encouragement. This monumental restoration idea of mine was admittedly well beyond your comfort zone, but you trusted in me and gave me the wings to soar. I threw everything but the kitchen sink at you - and when I got a sponsor for that, I threw that at you as well! You have always said that I am the front man and you are the behind-the-scenes guy. So often I get the accolades because of our respective roles, but I know in my heart that you are the most crucial ingredient to the Mansion's success. Now, because of you, the Stetson Mansion will be a source of inspiration for generations to come. Well done, Michael, well done!

Special Thanks

To Dan White, our lead carpenter - for lack of a better title - who slowly over time unveiled his full capabilities. I have to say that you are the most honest, hard-working and dependable man I have ever met. Thank you for finding humor in our madness and for never saying it can't be done.

To Alice Atkins McCoy – you are a gift from God. Not only did you create beautiful kitchens for us, but you introduced us to an amazing cadre of artists, designers, and manufacturers. They came on board only because of your faith in us. We will never forget that gesture of love and confidence. Thank you for your friendship and guidance.

To Gerry Kotze, the man who brought the Mansion to life with paint. You were supposed to be at the Mansion for a month or two with your team, but then your team vanished. Not you, though. You continued and I never had any doubt that you would do just fine all by yourself and I was right. The Mansion looks amazing and you should be so proud of yourself. Thank you.

To Sue Ryan, one of the "famous three" who actually believed in our crazy over the top dreams for the Stetson Mansion from the very first day I met you. Not once did we have to convince you that we were absolutely serious or committed to the project. You will never fully realize how reassuring it was to have you in our corner. The sincerity of your support was topped only by the joy you expressed in our thousands of little successes, but the biggest bonus of all is that I now have the honor to call you my friend.

To all the tour guides and booking agents over the years who have led and/or booked the countless number of visitors from around the globe, I take my hat off to you. Thank you Debbie Pixley, Robin Markus, JoAnn Heinle and Sue Pearson. Your love and pride for the Stetson Mansion is very obvious and greatly appreciated.

I am especially grateful to Kent Morton and Bill Hall, who have practically been with us from the beginning, in one way or another. Thank you for taking this ride and helping turn my dreams for the Stetson Mansion into reality – I applaud you both!

"I believe that one of the most patriotic things we can do as a nation is to preserve and celebrate our history. This includes saving our historic homes, landmarks and sites from the ravages of time and neglect. For within these national treasures lie the legacies of our past and the inspiration for our future. Please, embrace and save our history."

-JT Thompson

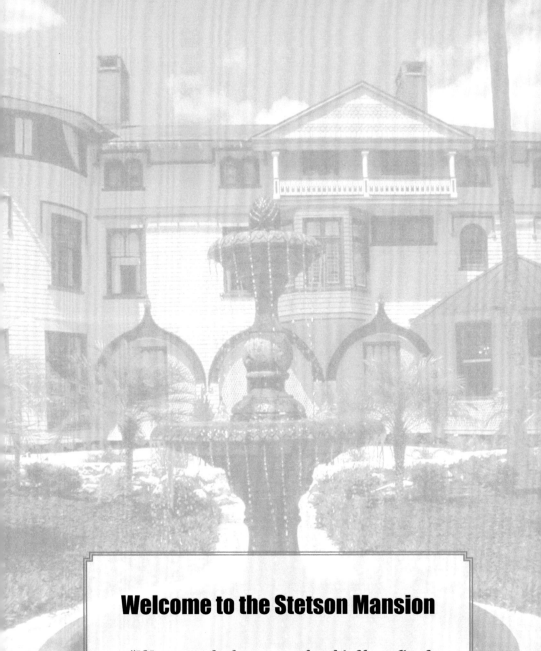

Welcome to the Stetson Mansion

"If I were asked to name the chief benefit of the house, I should say: the house shelters day-dreaming, the house protects the dreamer, the house allows one to dream in peace."

-Gaston Bachelard

Sometimes a house is more than just a house. Some homes provide a connective link to a nation's history. The Stetson Mansion is Florida's first luxury estate, but even more significantly, it is a vehicle for visitors from around the world to glance back in time and celebrate all the grandeur, innovation and excellence that we as a nation treasure.

Many of the great mansions built during the "Gilded Age" were blatant displays of conspicuous consumption. What makes the Stetson Mansion unique from many other Gilded Age estates is that it is not a display of conspicuous consumption, but instead a magnificent, yet subtle work of art. John B. Stetson, along with the architect George T. Pearson, built the estate not to stroke Mr. Stetson's ego, but as a winter family home that brought some northern design and innovations to DeLand. Spectacular inlaid parquet floors grace each of the rooms and more than 10,000 panes of antique glass are found throughout its three stories. These are just two of the original preserved features that caused me to surrender my heart the day I first walked through the Mansion doors.

When my partner Michael and I began this journey of restoration, it was with a singular objective in mind – to breathe new life into a structure that we would eventually call our home. But as the Mansion's colorful and glorious past unfolded, we knew that it was going to be much, much more than that. This was our opportunity to preserve and share an American treasure with generations to come. For the first time in more than 125 years, the entire Stetson Mansion is open for anyone to tour and experience firsthand - an invitation once reserved only for society's most elite. The mansion was known for hosting grand parties and one can only imagine what it was like back then to experience the abundance and privilege of those select few. Well, the chance to step back in time is here and the mansion has been infused with a breath of fresh air so that each and every one of us can now have the opportunity to be guests at this American masterpiece, all the while realizing that anything is possible.

Please make a point to visit the Stetson Mansion if you are in the Orlando or the central Florida area. We would love to welcome you. But in the meantime, I hope you enjoy our story.

A vintage car parked in the courtyard, the North side of the mansion.

Is That the Hat Guy's Mansion?

"Make things right and the best they can be."

-John B. Stetson

One of the most iconic symbols of Americana recognized around the world is the Stetson cowboy hat. I thought about renaming the mansion "The Hat Guy's Mansion" because that is a question I am asked time after time. We recently went on a travel adventure to Europe, Russia, and Africa. Whenever I was asked what I did for a living, I would ramble on about the Stetson Mansion and eight out of ten people would ask the same question – "Is that the hat guy's mansion?"

So let me fill you in on the life of John Batterson Stetson. Born May 5, 1830 in Orange, New Jersey to parents Stephan Stetson and Susan Batterson Stetson, John was the seventh of 12 children. His father was a hatter by trade. As a boy, John Stetson worked with his father until John was diagnosed with tuberculosis and his doctor predicted he had only a short time to live. With his health in jeopardy, he decided to leave his father's hat-making business to explore the American West, believing it might be his only chance to see it.

In the West, the former hat-maker met cattle drivers, cowboys and prospectors while noticing the coonskin caps were favored by many of the gold seekers. He wondered whether fur-felt would work for a lightweight, all-weather hat suitable for the West in the 1860s.

While using the waterways near camp for his daily needs, John noted that whenever beavers came out of the water, they would shake their pelt and their fur would immediately be dry. That got him wondering if those pelts could be used to make his hats. So he trapped some beavers and used their fur. These hats became an instant success with the men he traveled throughout the west with. Even though his hats were a huge hit on the trail, John still felt like a complete failure, because his health and finances were no better off than when he started out on his adventure.

On his trek home, John came across a prospector who did hit it big in the gold mines, and the miner offered John a five dollar gold piece for his hat – that was his eureka moment. Continuing home, John asked friends and family for the necessary funds to open a storefront in Philadelphia to manufacture and sell his new style of hat. He purchased new tools, hired two men, and found the perfect location in town to start realizing his vision.

So, he soon began to construct and sell durable and wellmade hats from waterproof felt hats with high, open crowns and broad rims that kept the hot sun off the cowboys' faces, necks and shoulders. That hat, named "Boss of the Plains" was an instant hit with the men out west. John knew that there was also a great opportunity for growth with the upper class gentlemen of the cities, but he was aware that he would have to design a more refined style to suit their business and social lifestyle. He went on to design several different styles of casual, business and formal hats, such as "The Carlsbad" which is easily identified by the crease down the front. The company grew to manufacture all types of hats, including the iconic cowboy hat, fedoras, and even women's hats. Today, all of the company's hats are commonly referred to as Stetsons.

The John B. Stetson Company became the largest hat manufacturer in the world - making Stetson a household name, and its founder a very wealthy man. John Stetson was known for caring for his workers – Stetson made sure his employees had a clean, safe place to work and he also built a hospital for them, a park and houses for his thousands of employees. Every Christmas Mr. Stetson would set aside hundreds of thousands of dollars for toys, turkeys and bonuses. That was a huge sum of money back in the 1880's, but he always shared his good fortune with his loyal workers. During the last decades of his life, Stetson became quite a philanthropist. This was due in no small part to his third wife Elizabeth, who encouraged and prodded him to ensure his legacy by donating and supporting

This Jackson Walker Painting hangs in the beautiful
Volusia County Courthouse in downtown DeLand.

A vintage postcard from the early 1900's.

the arts, schools, and other charitable organizations. In the late 1880's, Mr. Stetson's physician suggested that he winter in a warmer climate due to his health issues. Stetson's good friend Henry DeLand suggested he visit him in the newly founded city which bears his name. John was immediately captivated with the area and decided to make DeLand his family's winter home. He purchased 300 acres from Dr. Gillen with the full intention of planting citrus groves. He then began construction of the Mansion which he would call home, however Stetson's much younger wife Elizabeth was not a huge fan of the Florida venture so when she came to DeLand during the construction phase she convinced her husband to scale down the mansion's original design to a mere shadow of his plans, leaving us today with a 9,000 square foot work of art.

It is reported that between the years of 1887 and 1906 the Stetsons hosted such notables as the Astors (John Jacob Astor was one of the many unfortunate victims aboard the Titanic), the Melons, the Vanderbilts, the Carnegies, Henry Flagler, Baron Frederick DeBary, Louis Comfort Tiffany, President Grover Cleveland, and King Edward VII (then Prince of Wales).

Another of Stetson's noteworthy friends was none other than one of the world's most well-known and prolific inventors, Thomas A. Edison, who actually supervised the electrical install at the mansion. In fact Stetson Mansion is one of the first homes in the entire world to be designed and built with Edison electricity.

John loved being at his beloved "Gillen" (the name which he gave the Mansion) so it seems only appropriate that he passed away at the home which he held so closely to his heart during his 20th winter stay, in 1906. The home Stetson built, including the school house where his two boys were educated, has been lovingly restored and now welcomes thousands of visitors from around the globe each year.

John B Stetson's mansion in Philadelphia. He called it Illdro.

Workers in the Stetson
Hat factory in Philadelphia

Henry DeLand

This is the rooftop of the original schoolhouse with the
orange groves pictured behind it.

We believe that this is either a picture of relatives or possibly workers
playing instruments just off to the side of the front porch.

One of Mr. Stetson's pet alligators sunning himself outside of the alligator pit. He had two alligators - Ponce and DeLeon.

Workers in the cane fields on Mr. Stetson's 300 acre estate.

Mr. Stetson's orange grove packing plant

Pineapples were also grown at the estate and all guests were given one as a welcoming and departing gift.

King Edward VII

President Cleveland

Thomas A. Edison

George W. Vanderbilt

Flagler Hall at Stetson University

John B Stetson Jr.

Henry Stetson

Home that John Stetson built for Elizabeth's parents in Indiana.

Stetson University in the 1890's

The side veranda at Mr Stetson's Philadelphia mansion.

Unfortunately these marble lions were long gone by the time we got here.

Front porch of the Stetson Mansion around 1890-1900.

This is the original South elevation of the mansion.

The mansion is being painted and having a new roof installed.

Here is a picture of a fair or celebration in downtown DeLand in the 1890's.

The Hat Maker's Wife

"Women will never be as successful as men because they have no wives to advise them."

-Dick Van Dyke

Elizabeth Stetson's influence and support throughout their marriage was responsible for many of the wonderful accomplishments with which her husband is identified. Most people have no idea that without Elizabeth's input many of the efforts accredited to her husband may have never come to be; most notably those associated with Stetson University.

When John Stetson chose to winter in DeLand and build a new home here, Elizabeth by all accounts was not overjoyed. She was not fond of the home her husband had built, the climate or the insects, but she did find one thing that agreed with her love of culture and education – Stetson University.

Called DeLand Academy at the time, the university was to become Elizabeth Stetson's lifelong project. The school often struggled in its formative years and Henry DeLand's ability to support the institution was hampered due to crop loss from a freeze in 1886. Thanks to Elizabeth's encouragement, John Stetson infused DeLand Academy with a desperately needed endowment. The amount was so significant that the board of directors later decided to change the name to John B. Stetson University.

Her continued support and generous donations to Stetson University as well as numerous other institutions clearly demonstrates Elizabeth's gift for giving was no small influence on her husband.

Other than her interest in the University, Elizabeth enjoyed studying foreign languages, playing the piano and reading books including history, economics, politics and theology.

After the passing of John Stetson in 1906, Elizabeth's life took a surprising turn when she married the Count of Santa Eulalia in 1908. Elizabeth Stetson had gone from simple Indiana girl to a Countess residing in Portugal.

Elizabeth Stetson and her new husband, Count Santa Eulalia.

Elizabeth Stetson

Elizabeth Hall at Stetson University is named after Elizabeth Stetson

In 1909 Elizabeth, the Countess of Santa Eulalia, returned to DeLand with her husband as honored guests at Stetson University's Presentation day. It was her first visit back since the death of Mr. Stetson. During this time, Elizabeth took the opportunity to make further generous donations to the university which helped in the construction of the Sampson Library and Conrad Hall. From 1922-1928 Elizabeth gave $65,000 to the university, the largest cash endowment by an individual at that time.

In addition to her contributions to Stetson University it should be noted that Elizabeth also contributed a great deal of financial support to the Art Museum in Philadelphia, the public library of Philadelphia and other libraries in several universities.

Elizabeth Stetson is truly an impressive and noteworthy woman whose deserved recognition is much overdue.

A Bit of My Story

"Whatever a person's mind dwells on intensely and with firm resolve, that is exactly what he becomes."

- Shankaracharya

Every morning when I wake up, I give thanks for the abundance of opportunities that have filled my life. I am especially thankful for the chance to share the magic of the Stetson Mansion with thousands of visitors from around the globe - and most of all for allowing me to call this masterpiece home.

So how did a poor kid from the projects of Newark, New Jersey come to own this spectacular estate? As I fill in some of the blanks, you will discover that I don't possess a particular skill set that would lend itself to this venture. But I do have a very vivid imagination and my favorite pastime is dreaming about all those "imagine if" scenarios.

The impact that parents have on their children is so far reaching, in all aspects of their lives, that I think it is necessary to give a brief background on the man and woman who influenced me so profoundly as I set forth on my road to self-discovery.

My father, James J. Thompson, was born August 21, 1924 to Irish immigrants. His mother fled Ireland because of religious persecution, married after she arrived in the United States and gave birth to four children. At the age of sixteen my dad desperately wanted to join the armed forces so he forged his mother's signature to enlist in the United States Marine Corps. He told me once that although his mother was extremely disappointed by what he did, she secretly was very proud of his patriotism and bravery. My dad served our country for ten years and fought in both WWII and the Korean War. Upon returning home from his tour of duty he decided that he wanted to become a public servant so he took the exams for the State Police, the Newark Police Department and the Newark Fire Department. He passed all three exams but ultimately decided to become a Newark police officer. Good move because he met my mom while on patrol during a St. Patrick's Day parade in 1958 and they married in 1959. He served on the police force for 32 years, retiring as a lieutenant. Many of those years were tumultuous just by the nature of the job but add Newark to the equation and the impact is multiplied tenfold. My oldest sister Debbie reminded me that in 1967, as the city almost imploded during the Newark riots, my dad had to leave my mom and all four of us kids for two weeks.

I desperately craved a strong father son bond with my dad but unfortunately that never came to be. Even so – I still learned some extremely valuable life lessons from him that will forever be etched in my psyche, such as being responsible and honoring my word. James J. Thompson passed away December 4, 2003.

Anna Marie (Judge) Thompson was born November 17, 1927. She also came from very humble beginnings. Both her parents were also Irish immigrants and they, like so many others, moved to the U.S.A for a chance at a better life. She was the 7th of eight children, all of whom were born and raised in a cold water flat in Newark, New Jersey. Money was always scarce in her family and when her father unexpectedly passed away in his early fifties all eight children had to quit school and go to work. She was in the fourth grade when she was forced to leave school. Hopes of getting married and raising a family of her own were put on hold when her sister was diagnosed with breast cancer and soon after died, leaving behind a husband and two small children. She promised her sister on her death bed that she would help raise them - and she did.

Finally at thirty two years of age she married my father in 1959. They had four children in four years and during that time she also suffered two miscarriages. Her life with my father was challenging to say the least and she remained a stay at home mom with no driver's license until her early forties. Then things changed, she got her driver's license and was hired by the Newark Board of Education as a teacher's aide for special

This is my mom around the age of 21. She looks like a star out of central casting in this photo.

My father served in the Marine Corps for 10 years. In this photo he is about 23 years old.

This is my mom and dad on their wedding day in 1959.

needs children. That career lasted almost fifteen years and she touched the lives of thousands of little boys and girls.

My mom, my hero, my biggest fan passed away on August 28, 2011. There is not a day that goes by that I do not think about or miss her. Anna M. Thompson was a dynamo. She taught me so much by the virtue of how she lived her life:
- Never take yourself too seriously – and remember you're never too old for me to knock some sense into you.
- Fear and adversity are best fought with will power and perseverance, so cut the crap and get back to work.
- When you stop dreaming or expecting miracles you might as well get the shovel, dig a ditch and jump in.

She definitely had a way with words. I am honored to call her mom and friend. Her spirit will forever reside in my soul.

I was born August 24, 1964 in Newark, New Jersey as the youngest of four children and the only boy. My first ten years of life in the housing projects of Newark provided numerous challenges. Survival depended on your ability to roll with the punches, and let me tell you - there were plenty of those to roll with. Early on my family nicknamed me "dreamer" because I would get so lost in my own thoughts that I sometimes became oblivious to my surroundings. Whether it was my mom calling me ten times before I was even aware of her existence or me continually being late for school because I missed my bus stop by ten to fifteen blocks. My imagination would sometimes take over my mind and lead me on adventures of "impossible" dreams. Those "imagine if" mental vacations helped me to cope with some hard times, but more importantly they gave me a glimpse into a world of possibility. Many would call it fantasy or wishful thinking at best. My parents would very often tell me to stop dreaming and focus, but for whatever reason I felt at home in that world of make believe. Reality was a little over-rated for me!

My first grade school picture.

This is me wearing my dad's Stetson. He wore a hat every Sunday to church and on special occasions.

My father and I circa 1976.

This picture of my mother and I is from the 1980's. The hair is always a dead giveaway.

This is Bradley Court, the housing projects that I was born and raised in till the age of 11.

The Newark riots made national headlines and my dad was in the heart of it as a Newark police officer.

These are my sisters Debbie and Terri. They always had to keep their eyes on me because I was continually wandering off or daydreaming.

My three sisters and I putting in our requests with Santa.

46

Eventually we moved out of the projects into a real house with a yard and a garage. We really hit it big! I completed high school and attended one year of community college. For the next 20 years I did anything and everything when it came to employment. I seemed to be drawn to opportunities that I knew little to nothing about. I owned a deli-convenience store, I got involved with multi-level marketing, I was a buyer for men's clothing, and I even owned a tropical fish business. There was no rhyme or reason for my decisions. The driving force was the need for success. In hindsight my business choices, while not always sound, were invaluable lessons for the journey ahead. Even when the ventures were epic disasters, pearls of wisdom could be found hidden within. I just had to be willing to sift through the rubble to find them.

During these times of me trying to figure out life's secrets I met a girl in Florida named Laurie and we became good friends, then best friends and after a few years and some hurdles along the way we fell in love and were married in New Jersey in 1991. We eventually moved back to Florida in 1992 and not to long after, became proud parents of a beautiful, healthy, strong willed baby boy – Austin Hunter Thompson born June 4, 1994. The moment he came into this world he stole my heart and gave me a whole new perspective on life, which sounds so cliché but it is absolutely true. Laurie and I later divorced but much to her credit we still remain friends 18 years later. I speak for both of us when I say Austin is our pride and joy.

Laurie, Austin and I on the day of his christening.

Every now and then I would take a nap with my little guy because he kept me going non-stop.

Austin at one year old. I tried to prepare him for the business world early and was teaching him to dress for success.

Austin posing for his Christmas pictures.

Austin and I sporting our Barcelona wool hats that I picked up on
one of our getaways. Barcelona is one of my favorite European cities
and I can't wait to take Austin there one day.

Every now and then Michael will pry me away from working and force
me to go out and paint the town.

Fast forward several years, jobs, and businesses later, and, hello Stetson Mansion. After years of searching for what would bring success, I finally tapped into what so many "successful people" had been advocating over the years: "Do what you love and the money will follow." These words drove me crazy at the time, but when I finally stopped chasing the dollar, my life transformed at lightning speed. I wasted so much time searching for a more profound and complex formula to success, when doing what you love to do was the secret to success all along. Not much of a secret at all. What I loved was transforming buildings – I realized that I loved turning run-down structures from eyesores to eye candy.

Michael and I restored several small houses and a twenty-unit motel together – all in south Florida. We were very successful, but even more importantly for me, I found something about which I was passionate and it energized me. The bonus was that what we were doing inspired others as well, whether it was a neighbor making an extra effort to spruce up his or her home or other investors who followed suit. The ripple effect was far-reaching.

This became the foundation on which the Stetson Mansion renovation would build upon. I hope this glimpse into my life serves as proof-positive that anyone can achieve success. Few guarantees exist in life but I have found that choosing more powerful thoughts will propel you towards your dreams and goals faster than you can imagine –guaranteed! Life is meant to be a downstream adventure. Let your words, thoughts, and dreams be your lifeboat.

This view of the mansion is absolutely breathtaking. The reflection of light and movement on the antique windows always reminds me of those moments as you are coming out of a dream state.

Ready...Go!

"Without a sense of urgency, desire loses its value."

- John Rohn

There was always a sense of urgency, on my part, with anything involving the Stetson Mansion. The minute we first saw a picture of it at the realtor's office in 2005, I had to see it immediately despite the fact that the Mansion was nothing at all what we were looking for in a second home. We were in the Daytona Beach and Flagler Beach areas looking at 1,200 to 1,500 square foot cottages all within a block of the ocean – that's all. Never once did we consider a home this large - especially not a Victorian mansion listed on the National Historic Register. But after not finding anything to my liking, I asked our realtor if she had anything with "a little more character." Be very careful what you ask for in life!

The Stetson Mansion was the third or fourth property we saw on the computer screen and it immediately caught my eye. How could it not - it was enormous, beautiful, and perfect! Ok, so maybe not perfect at all, but what a first impression. It was almost as if it called out to me, "Don't pass me by, save me!" I remember the experience like it was yesterday. Now while the Mansion was begging to be rescued, Michael was pleading to move on to the next page. "Absolutely not JT, that is way too big and nowhere near the ocean. Not to mention an enormous money pit. No way, forget about it!"

This is how the mansion looked just before we purchased it. The huge blank space on the left drove me crazy!

This is the north side of the mansion as it appeared when we first visited.

Back of the mansion, the east side. This sliding glass door is no longer here.

South view of the mansion. The vines may have been strangling the palm trees but they were killing me!

After we got here I removed the chain link fence around the pool area to make it easier to mow but the vines and weeds were definitely taking over this entire area.

This is what the reception parlor looked like when we first walked in. This is not the original wallpaper and even though it was not horrible it fought with the room so it had to go.

I had a vision for the kitchen the very first time I saw it. This is the beginning of the demo.

This is what the now Elizabeth Suite looked like before I tore down the wallpaper and changed the light fixture. Although this is an original Edison light fixture I hated it. Sorry Mr. Edison. Don't worry we have it in storage.

The third floor was a disaster. The floors were painted with a red muddy paint and this was the wallpaper used in the two middle rooms – black with colored poppies.

This is the South side of the mansion. All the plumbing was on the outside and was a true sign of prosperity in Victorian times.

This was the old garage that was attached to the mansion when we arrived, built in the 1970's.

The front of the original schoolhouse.

The rear of the schoolhouse required us to add many new shingles to fill the boarded up openings.

I remained undeterred in my enthusiasm, however, and when we finally got inside the Mansion after having to wait two days for the owners to return home from vacation, the journey began. I walked six feet through the front doors and turned to Michael and said, "This is going to be our home." So much for playing it cool and uninterested! It was almost as if the house chose us and did everything in its power not to let us go.

Every room that I walked into stole another piece of my heart. I became oblivious to any disrepair or renovation challenge. I saw only the beauty and potential. Michael's experience was slightly different. Yes, he did recognize many of the architectural elements and treasures – especially the floors and windows, but he was overwhelmed by the scope and vastness of the unfathomable renovation. Every time I turned to him for his reaction I saw the "money pit" look in his eyes. I knew I was going to need a lot of help winning him over to my side.

I remained relentlessly enthusiastic and I pulled out every weapon I had in my arsenal to make my case. I wore him down and he realized it was futile to try to thwart my obsession with the Mansion. We made an offer the next day and several months later we were the proud owners of a mansion 26 miles away from the ocean and 9,000 square feet more than we ever wanted. Stetson Mansion was nothing that we had hoped for, but everything we could ever dream of. Now the real fun would begin.

Michael snapped this picture of the mansion as we were leaving after our second visit. I never saw the flaws only the potential. There was no turning back for me by this time – the spell was cast.

COBBLE SYSTEMS PRESENTS

THE

STETSON MANSION

DESIGNER SHOWCASE
AND EXHIBITION

A Partnership To Benefit
The Museum Of Florida Art
www.MuseumofFloridaArt.com

HOSTED BY

Alice Atkins McCoy

You Wanna Do What?

"I think being different, going against the grain in society, is the greatest thing in the world."

-Elijah Woods

This was amazing! We were now the proud owners of this architectural masterpiece and it was bigger than all the homes we had ever renovated – combined. What were we thinking? We did not have the large amount of funds required to renovate this monster.

The Mansion had a number of owners over the years, but the large property was expensive to keep up in its original condition and it had deteriorated considerably. The last family that owned the Mansion lived here for 28 years and they had maintained the estate to the best of their means. The "bones" of the house and some of its most magnificent elements such as the floors and windows had survived the years. That being said, it needed a major overhaul. The roof on the Mansion was probably a year away from being compromised by water – we got here just in time.

Sometimes out of desperation comes one's greatest inspiration. I decided to turn the Mansion renovation into an opportunity for a designer and manufacturers' showcase - an idea I had five minutes after I saw the Mansion for the first time in the realtor's office. At the time I even jumped up out of my chair and announced it to all present. Michael told me to sit down because I was sounding crazy. The realtor suggested I save my enthusiasm and brainstorming until after I had seen the property. On the ride home from the realtor's, Michael asked me, "Why would anyone want to participate in a showcase for the Stetson Mansion?" And my response was, "Why wouldn't everyone want to participate?"

I called and spoke with a producer at Home and Garden Television and told them about the Mansion and my brilliant showcase idea. Who knows? Maybe they would want to document the restoration. The woman asked me several questions and then asked me what other projects or showcase homes I had done before, as well as what exactly I expected. "I don't want money," I said. "I only want product and possibly designers and artisans to donate goods and services." I also admitted that I had no experience soliciting sponsors and had never been involved with a showcase home. She was very kind and ultimately more helpful than she will ever know, but her snickering response to my idea was, "Oh, is that all you want?"

Everyone I spoke with about the showcase seemed to have the same mantra – "You wanna do what?" Some people, including local elected officials, chuckled at my naïve and seemingly doomed idea. "Why would anyone want to 'give' you product to restore your own home?" I was asked this question a thousand times at least. I tried to explain that no one was giving us anything for "free." Sponsors were offered the opportunity to display their products or highlight their services in a spectacular historic mansion that would be seen by thousands and thousands of visitors during a three-month showcase. Not to mention the hundreds of thousands of online viewers who would visit the Stetson Mansion website. I knew I wasn't a "name" in the industry, so I offered an unusually long showcase to make up for that. Most showcases are available to the public for less than a month.

"Ok, let's say you get all these sponsors to go along with your plan - who is going to come to DeLand, Florida?" "Does anyone even know what the Stetson Mansion is?" "Better yet, does anyone even know who John B. Stetson was?" We were up against this type of skepticism throughout the entire process. In the beginning, only three people supported or believed in us – three people! To this day, I am floored how I managed to maintain my determination to save and restore the Mansion in the midst of such adversity. My blinders remained on at all times and my frequency tuned only into what supported my beliefs and goals.

I worked so hard on trying to clean up the mansion before I allowed any sponsors to come see it. I did not want them to be overwhelmed by the scope of the restoration but instead be wowed by the architecture.

I was always excited about seeing work get done. This is a picture of the hallway that now houses the famous Edison circuit box.

I can't come to the phone I am all tied up!

I made it my mission to tell the world John B. Stetson's role in American cultural and economic history and how his winter mansion was the epitome of American exceptionalism. I started calling everybody - manufacturers, artists, designers, retailers, newspapers, magazines, TV stations, radio stations, and anyone else who would listen.

Against all odds, Michael and I enrolled more than 325 sponsors from around the country and Canada. Some potential sponsors received more than 100 voicemails until they finally called me back. They say that the squeaky wheel gets the oil, but the squeaky 18-wheeler gets a lot more!

Alice Atkins McKoy was a Godsend. She was responsible for us getting some of our largest sponsors. She is also one of the few female certified master kitchen and bath designers in the state of Florida. Everyone should have an Alice by their side when they are designing a kitchen or bath.

When I got Michael to agree to purchase the Stetson Mansion, part of the deal was that he would not have to supervise the renovation. I assured him that I would have no problem finding the perfect person to handle the task. Send in the architects, builders, and historians, and let's get this thing started. Despite my optimism and enthusiasm, the pool of interviewed candidates reached a general consensus that the Mansion restoration would take approximately five to seven years to complete. Five to seven years? I wanted to be done in a year! One contractor-architect told me that I was insane and that I had completely unrealistic expectations. Another architect told me that he would have to sit with the project for at least six months before he started any actual work. All I wanted was for the work to start and the restoration to move along at a reasonable pace. What's unreasonable about that? My favorite advice though was from a "noted" architect who suggested that I may want to consider putting the Mansion back up for sale so that someone who knows what they are doing could buy it before I destroy it. Needless to say we didn't hire any of them!

I had never hired anyone for this type of project before, so I was forced to ask Michael to take on what I promised him he would never have to do. I broke the news to him about my failed attempts to hire a contractor or architect and that he was the only person with whom I was comfortable to supervise the entire renovation. I then immediately checked his vital signs and they weren't looking so good.

As I saw it, no one loved or knew this house better than we did. We had inspected every square inch of the three-story Mansion as well as the original schoolhouse built behind the main house for educating John and Elizabeth Stetson's two sons. We knew every room and every floor, door and window in this place. I admit it, I fell head over heels in love with the Mansion and there was no way I was going to fail to bring it back to its original glory. So I knew in my heart that the restoration had to be supervised by someone who had *almost* as much passion and love for the Mansion as I did. Sorry, Michael, but it was your destiny to be at the helm!

How long did the restoration finally take? With Michael supervising workers and me driving us to the brink of insanity with 12-16 hour days, we completed most of the restoration in 18 months.

Anything is possible when you tell yourself anything is possible! The story I continually told myself ended only in success – failure was never considered as an option. At least not for me.

Inspiration at Every Turn

"If I have seen further than others, it is by standing upon the shoulders of giants."

- Isaac Newton

One thing never in short supply at the Mansion was inspiration. From the original Thomas Edison circuit box and lighting fixtures to the dozens of intricate inlaid parquet patterns or the stained and leaded glass windows that changed from room to room, beauty encapsulated the Stetson Mansion. The architectural features dictated an overall theme and feel in each of the rooms which was very helpful in collaborating with the many artists and designers who participated in the renovation and showcase. Luckily, we worked with some exceptionally talented people who never let their designs or finishes compete for the spotlight. Their work only enhanced the already beautiful spaces.

But this was just the superficial inspiration of the Mansion. A much deeper almost spiritual inspiration exists that you are only privy to when you spend more time here. The superficial beauty of the Mansion is breathtaking to say the least, but that is just the most obvious layer. The deeper invisible layer that can only be reached through the senses is heart stirring and sometimes even overpowering. From the very first day I stepped foot into the Mansion, I was spellbound.

I am a big believer in synchronicity - those moments that just so perfectly collide with one another and remind us that there are angels conspiring on our behalf. Moments of synchronicity occurred regularly at the Mansion which was yet another vehicle of inspiration for me. I have only shared what I am about to relate with a handful of people. After we closed on the Mansion, I spent several months in the house alone. Michael was forced to tend to other business we had in south Florida thanks to hurricane Wilma.

I was so anxious to get my hands on the Mansion that I started work immediately. While I was ripping down wallpaper and knocking down walls I could not help but feel someone was

These are the stained glass windows that grace the "grand" staircase. I never get tired of looking at them.

This is the original Edison circuit box that operated much of the electricity in the mansion up until 2006.

The inlaid parquet floors at the Stetson Mansion are spectacular. The designs change from room to room and floor to floor and many of the designs are three dimensional. These are some of the most beautiful and intricate parquet floors in the world.

with me. This was not a spooky or scary feeling – just a sense that I was not alone. So I convinced myself that it was John B. Stetson. I began talking to him constantly when I was at the Mansion. I would inform him of my plans and share my dreams with him. As I walked down the hallways I would turn and speak to him as if he was walking behind me. I had a sense of complete confidence with my choices because I believed I had the approval of the man himself. Now for those who may be worried about my mental health and want to refer me to a good psychiatrist, thank you, but I'll pass. For everyone else, welcome to my world of inspiration.

I always say that the Mansion resides in a vortex of love, possibility, and inspiration. So far I have no reason to believe otherwise, and even if I did, I would ignore it.

For the record, I still have my talks with John B, and something tells me he approves of what we have done.

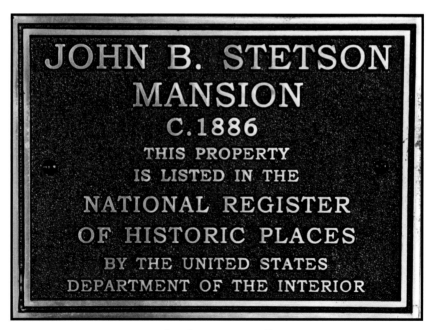

The plaque says it all.

Here They Come!

"The greatest pleasure in life is doing what people say you cannot do."

- Walter Bagehot

We actually did it! The Stetson Mansion was officially ready for its first tour. More than a year and a half of planning, organizing, enrolling, supervising, promoting, arguing, and stressing, and now the doors were ready to be opened for all the world to see.

Michael and I decided that we would donate 100% of the proceeds from the showcase to the community and we chose the Florida Museum of Art's children's youth programs to receive the funds. The fit was perfect because we love children and in our eyes the Mansion was one of Florida's greatest works of art.

What if the people who knew best were right? What if no one came to tour the Mansion? Did I let my enthusiasm and passion for the Mansion take over all rational thinking? Absolutely! I let my imagination run wild like I did when I was a seven year old boy in the projects – when I thought anything was possible. My dreams possessed and intoxicated me and I lived as if they had already come true the moment I created them two years earlier.

Guess what? Before long they did come true! One day like magic the Mansion was ready for its close-up. The key to the magic, at least my brand of magic, lies within the thoughts in which we choose to believe. I believed that the world needed to experience the Mansion and I thought of every possible reason why it would happen. The showcase was a huge success and we raised tens of thousands of dollars for the Museum's children's programs.

Many naysayers told me that my ideas were way too grandiose and that I would be lucky if I could attract a couple of hundred visitors to the Mansion. Finally they were right about something! My dreams were definitely grandiose and I was lucky to attract a couple of hundred visitors – in the first few days!

We had planned a three-month showcase after which we would close the doors of the Mansion to the public and live a quiet, normal life once again. Yeah right! First of all, I am not very good at living the quiet life and secondly, there is nothing normal about me. The showcase was such a huge success and touched and inspired so many people that we could not bring ourselves to close it after 90 days. So we decided to continue for a little longer. That "little longer" is still going on and every year more and more visitors come to experience the magic and grandeur of the Stetson Mansion first hand. Every time I am blessed enough to lead a tour, I get to relive that first day when the Mansion doors opened and the love affair began. The magic never ends!

We work so hard to make every visitor feel like they are a special guest at the mansion and our TripAdvisor reviews reflect that commitment.

One of our very first tours.

Sharing the mansion with guests from around the globe is an absolute joy for me.

We all get so excited to see buses parked in front of the Mansion. One day soon we will be welcoming hundreds of buses a year to the estate.

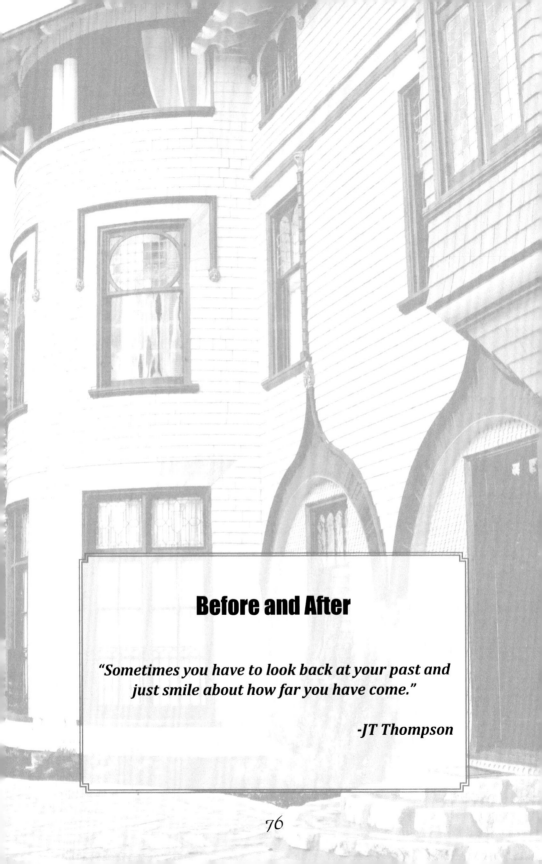

Before and After

"Sometimes you have to look back at your past and just smile about how far you have come."

-JT Thompson

Ok, I know I can't be the only one who loves looking at before and after pictures of restorations. This is my definition of instant gratification. There is something so comforting about seeing an immediate transformation right before your eyes. I don't care if the caption says that it took 19 years to painstakingly complete the project, the after picture is instantaneous! Thousands and thousands of visitors have toured the Stetson Mansion and one of the most frequently asked questions on our tours is, "Do you have any before pictures?"

Michael and I worked at such a frenzied pace that we barely had time to take pictures. Some days we only got to see each other as we passed in the hallways during our 16 hour shifts. Needless to say we don't have nearly as many photos as we would both like and most of the ones that we do have are due to Michael's insistence as well as some awesome photographers along the way. Even so, sorting through file after file of pictures for this book was mind boggling to say the least because I was reminded about just how much we accomplished. Sometimes you really do have to look back to realize just how far you have traveled.

There was no access on this side of the mansion so Michael had custom French doors built to fit the opening. The center window that was removed was installed in the kitchen.

We added a fountain, a natural stone patio, painted the mansion with a bolder paint scheme using six different colors and installed all new landscaping. This area is now used quite often for parties, events and weddings.

The schoolhouse was built just for the Stetson boys to be taught in during their winter stay. Over the years it had many uses but when we got here, it was in sad shape.

This is what the schoolhouse looks like now.

There were bars on all the windows and an old propane tank right next to the building.

We added a small patio so that the schoolhouse really felt like a separate little home. The shutters give it a romantic feel and they are also hurricane rated.

I fell in love with this building the second I stepped inside. I saw it completely done in my head within minutes. Michael wasn't quite as taken by it and in fact he wanted to turn it into a shed/storage building.

The schoolhouse had to be jacked up because it was completely lopsided and the floors were all replaced as well. All the walls ceilings and windows are original but we did add the hand hewn beam and the side door.

Tah-dah! Our very own Zen- like retreat featuring the original soaring Polynesian ceiling. Guests are always surprised how spacious the schoolhouse is when they first walk in.

This garage was added on by the previous owners and there was never any doubt in my mind that it was going to be torn down.

Two guys demolished the garage using a chain saw and a sledge hammer and then hauled it away in their pick-up truck.

Michael and I purchased the plans for the carriage house on line and had an architect modify them to our exact specifications.

Carriage house blends in perfectly. We installed a metal roof to add a little more interest.

Whenever Michael and I purchase a property the first thing I do is strip the landscape of all the crap so that I have a fresh clean canvass to work with. I find blank pages inspirational.

This is the result. This picture was taken at dusk and doesn't the warm glow emanating from the windows make you want to peek inside?

This was what the front of the mansion looked like before we moved in.

We added shutters to the blank space above the porch which balances the front elevation. Now it actually looks like the front of the mansion.

This is one of the carpenters installing our custom balustrades that are copied from a 19th century mansion.

The porch is now more like an outside room - an extension of the mansion. There is no better place in the world to relax with a nice cold John B Stetson Bourbon Mint Julep. Life is good!

Most of the palm trees at the estate are over 120 years old. Seeing the vines taking over the trees drove me crazy. I could not wait to free them from being strangled.

The south elevation as it appears currently at the mansion.

A lot of people refer to this as the front of the mansion but it's not. We ripped out over 1,000 linear feet of chain link fencing from around the property and hundreds of bushes and weed trees.

Today the mansion is surrounded by black metal estate fencing and beautiful healthy bushes.

The pool area began to look like it was hidden in the jungle.

We installed a retainer wall and added over 1,500 square feet to the deck area. Here is the newly pavered deck and the pool ready for the new liner.

We kept the pool area somewhat simple, but when we first arrived we were considering relocating it in the courtyard area or the south lawn.

Stetson University hosted their new president's welcome reception at the mansion. Dr. Wendy Libby is now at the helm.

This is what the mansion looked like after the first day the painters left.

This is what it looked like several weeks after they finished.

Michael surprised me one weekend while I was away. He removed all the exterior plumbing that was on the mansion and brought it inside where it belongs.

Now all you see is beautiful architecture. Look at those windows!

I ripped down a couple of hundred rolls of wallpaper throughout the mansion. After spending months doing that by myself I swore I would never hang paper in the mansion ever again. This was the design in the reception parlor.

I went to many garage sales, auctions and estate sales in the beginning and I found some really great deals. Here are some of those deals in the alcove area of the reception parlor.

This is what the reception parlor transformed into. Good lighting makes such a difference in a room.

The music room/library area had no access to the outside which closed off this side of the mansion to entertaining. The original walls were in great condition but the ugly radiator had to go.

The Gothic glass wall is gorgeous and thank God it was in great condition.

We use this room all the time, and it is great for parties or watching movies. Many of our guests and visitors feel they are walking on a work of art.

This was how the dining room looked
when we first saw it.

This is the how it looked after we moved in but before the renovation.

There were so many layers of flooring in the kitchen and the last layer took days to get off.

Here's Michael taking up some carpet strips. The brick next to him is original and was covered in a plaster mixture which took both of us two weeks to chip off.

This is the Elizabeth suite in the midst of the restoration.

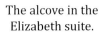

The alcove in the Elizabeth suite.

I thought that the bed should be in the alcove of the Elizabeth suite, and guess what, I got my way!

I didn't have many pictures of the master bedroom. After removing the
wallpaper I have to come back and scrape off all the backing.
Worst job ever!

The master bedroom today. Notice the three dimensional floors.

This is what the master bathroom looked liked when we came on board. We gave this claw foot tub to one of our sponsors as our way of saying thank you. This was not the original claw foot tub, it is from the 1920's or 1930's.

This is the first stage of our master bathroom renovation.

This is what the master bath looks like today. The mural was done by one of the top 200 muralists in the world.

Master Bath

This is what the servants staircase looked like after years of wear and tear. This is the staircase that we use all the time.

There are small leaded glass windows perfectly placed up the staircase so that the natural light fills the hallway and gives you a chance to peer out along the way.

The third floor hallway was in desperate need of some tlc.

This is how it looks now.

This is what the Governess Suite looked like when we came on board.

The Governess Suite is now often referred to as the Sky Suite because of the mural. This is a favorite room of many of our guests.

This is what the Garden Suite looked like after we cleaned it up.

This is what the Garden Suite looks like after the complete restoration.

Every room in the mansion was used as a storage area at one time or another during the restoration. Here you can see the Balcony Suite waiting to be cleared out.

The transformation was incredible and the balcony is a great spot to start or end your day.

Stetson Mansion
Photo Gallery

The dining room is now a welcoming and elegantly designed room that anyone would love to dine in. The beautiful leaded glass windows are all original to 1886.

The Balcony Suite is my favorite room in the mansion. When I was a little boy growing up in the housing projects I always dreamed that one day I would build the coolest tree house around with its very own own lookout tower. It took me over forty years - but this is my tree house.
Some things are so worth the wait!

The kitchen is the heart of the home and I love to cook so I had a huge input in this space. I insisted on these oversized pendants and the crimson colored professional appliances.

I designed this Christmas tree in celebration of my mom's life the year she passed away.

These are a Few of My Favorite Things

"We lose ourselves in the things we love.
We find ourselves there too."

-Kristin Martz

The Stetson Mansion is a treasure trove of beautiful things all wrapped up in one big spectacular package. I could fill the pages of multiple books detailing all that I love or am inspired by at the Mansion. Whether it is the "Gilded Age" craftsmanship of the floors, the innovation of Edison's work or any of the new additions to the mansion, the list is endless. The best part of all is that the list keeps growing and growing. Here are just a few of my favorite "things" that fill my days with bursts of inspiration and joy. You can see why I live in such a state of gratitude.

I purchased this at an auction and the story is unbelieveable. I'll tell you all about it when you get here!!

I love this window because it reminds me of the "magic mirror" from the kids tv show "Romper Room."

This wall is from a French Chateau ca. 1770's – 1790's with all the original glass.

These oversized kitchen pendants are some of my favorite new additions at the mansion.

It's so hard to choose a favorite floor but this one is a contender.

This hallway always shimmers because of the copper leafing and crushed embedded glass on the ceiling.

Another great view from the Gillen Suite.

One of my favorite
celebs wearing a Stetson.

I always wanted a lake at
the mansion and thanks to
photoshop I can have one.

Disney has Mickey Mouse and
we have Manny Mouse.

So far this is the only picture
we have found of John B wearing
a Stetson.

This was the very first couple to be married at the mansion and they just so happened to be our really good friends.

This brides expression defines
the meaning of true love.

This photo is the perfect blend of East meets West.

I decorate about 20+ Christmas trees at the mansion every year and this was my woodland themed tree. This tree cost me under $25 to decorate.

This is my favorite alcove at the mansion, which is in the Stetson Suite. This is also the master suite and I was told that this was one of Mr Stetson's favorite spots to read.

My favorite piece of outdoor art. Talk about attitude – look at that peacock's face.

Michael designed this Torii , a Japanese gate, for the entrance into the meditation garden that I designed. I am so fortunate to have this getaway.

This is one of my favorite crown molding designs in the mansion. Mr. Stetson made sure to place double fleur dis les heart on this beam so that when ever Elizabeth looked up she would be reminded that he loves her twice as much as anyone else in the world.

The" Gatsby" bathroom is named such because of its 1920's styling. This is my second favorite bathroom but for many guests it is their first choice. Thank God we have over a dozen to choose from!

Don't Dream Big... Dream Gigantic!

"Cut not the wings of your dreams, for they are the heartbeat and the freedom of your soul."

-Flavia

When we began the restoration of the Stetson Mansion, we knew that we were in for the ride of a lifetime. What we didn't expect though was that this adventure would present us with a key that would open up a whole new world of possibilities for our community and for ourselves.

Stetson Mansion was a diamond that had been forgotten in time. It was desperately crying out for the right person or persons to see past the decades of neglect and save it. This diamond desperately needed to be polished. I had never polished a diamond before, but I have never been one to run from a challenge. We took on the task in hopes that the Mansion would once again sparkle like it did in the 19th century. Mission accomplished! Stetson Mansion now shines even brighter in the 21st century. She is grander and more beautiful than ever before and has taken her rightful place as the "crown jewel" of central Florida.

So many of our nation's architectural treasures have been lost to the wrecking ball to make way for progress and development. I strongly believe and support growth and capitalism, but not at the expense of our soul – our history. Unfortunately, we have become such a disposable society. Not perfect – tear it down. Too much money, time, and effort to restore – get rid of it. We are such a young nation, but we have erased so much of our history and heritage in small towns and big cities across the country. We have to stop being so shortsighted. Michael and I would not allow the Stetson Mansion to fall victim to shortsighted economic gain. Structures like this have a priceless intrinsic value because they stand as beacons to remind us of where we came from and how connected we all are in some ways. They are like sacred time capsules that hold and preserve our history and culture within their walls. One day future generations will explore these places to discover their pasts and inspire their futures.

So there you have it – that's how you polish a diamond!

I hope that my words have given you some insight into this glorious place I get to call home – the Stetson Mansion. I feel incredibly blessed to wake up every day knowing that I will soon be welcoming visitors from around the world through our front doors. I still get excited when I see the crowds gather and people roaming the grounds just before a tour. My level of enthusiasm today is the same as it was for my very first tour. Visitors think that they are here to see a beautiful Victorian mansion – and they will not be disappointed. But I know there is so much more!

I don't know what the next chapter will be in my life's story, but I do know that I look forward to challenging myself with new and even more exciting goals, dreams, and adventures. Stetson Mansion will forever be part of my soul as well as a constant point of reference on the journey ahead. The future of the Mansion is brighter than ever and I look forward to the day when it becomes a source of pride and inspiration on a much larger national and international scale. I don't think that day is very far away.

Thank you so much for allowing me to share my story with you. I hope that somewhere tucked in between all my words you were able to see my heart and that I conveyed just how appreciative and grateful I truly am for this abundant life of mine. Good luck to all you other dreamers out there and remember – don't just dream big – dream GIGANTIC!

See you at the Mansion!!

Credits

Editor - Sue Ryan
Elizabeth's story - Written by Rosa Meddaugh
Cover Design - Nicole Pacheco

Photo Credits
Michael Solari
Edson Pacheco ~ Karrah Flores
Tina Aten ~ Allen Whitson
Seth Benson ~ Norman Yu
Stetson University Archives

CITY OF ORLANDO

Proclamation

WHEREAS, in May of 2014, the Stetson Mansion was named the most popular tourist attraction in Florida by TripAdvisor, the world's largest travel site; and

WHEREAS, the Stetson Mansion was built in 1886 by famed hat maker and philanthropist John B. Stetson to serve as his winter retreat; and

WHEREAS, the Stetson Mansion at 10,000 square feet, is Florida's first luxury home and is regarded as one of America's top 300 historic homes; and

WHEREAS, the Stetson Mansion eclectic and unusual design includes various carvings, 10 of the nation's most intricate parquet wood floor patterns, 10,000 panes of leaded glass windows, the most unusual feature, a fully up to date infrastructure, as well as furnishings that blend the past with the present in a seamless celebration of classic elegance with fresh design; and

WHEREAS, this recognition will result in an increase in tourism to DeLand and the greater Orlando area; and

WHEREAS, we extend our congratulations to JT Thompson and Michael Solari, the owners of the Stetson Mansion who have worked so hard to make the visitor's experience at Stetson Mansion memorable; and

WHEREAS, we extend our thanks for the business that the Stetson Mansion has generated for others in the greater Orlando and Central Florida area;

NOW, THEREFORE, I, BUDDY DYER, Mayor of the City of Orlando, hereby do proclaim Sunday, August 24, 2014 as

"Stetson Mansion Day"

in the City of Orlando.

IN WITNESS WHEREOF, I hereunto have set my hand and caused the Seal of the City of Orlando to be affixed this 24th day of August 2014.

MAYOR

σ

Proclamation

The CITY OF DELAND
Volusia County, Florida

Certificate of Recognition

Whereas, the Stetson Mansion has been named Florida's Most Popular Attraction for 2014 by TripAdvisor.com; and

Whereas, the Stetson Mansion was built in 1886 by famed hat maker and philanthropist John B. Stetson which served as his winter retreat and the Stetson Mansion at 10,000 square feet is Florida's first luxury home and is regarded as one of America's top 300 historic homes, and;

Whereas, the eclectic and unusual design includes not only various complicated carvings but 10 of the nation's most rare and intricate parquet wood floor patterns, 10,000 panes of leaded glass windows and the most unusual feature of having fully up to date infrastructure and furnishings that blend the past and present in a seamless celebration of classic elegance with fresh design; and

Whereas, this recognition will result in even greater positive impacts than currently generated by the Stetson Mansion on tourism in DeLand and West Volusia resulting in more visitors to enjoy all that DeLand and West Volusia has to offer; and

Whereas, we extend our congratulations to J.T. Thompson and Michael Solari, the owners of the Stetson Mansion who have worked so hard to make the visitors' experience at Stetson Mansion memorable and our thanks for the business that their success has generated for others in our City.

Now, therefore, I, Robert F. Apgar, Mayor of the City of DeLand, and on behalf of the City Commission extend our congratulations to the Stetson Mansion, and its owners J.T. Thompson and Michael Solari for being recognized as Florida's Most Popular Attraction for 2014 and urge all our citizens to recognize the Stetson Mansion as a valuable historic resource. Further, we acknowledge the significance of this recognition for our community and the positive impact it will have on tourism in DeLand and West Volusia benefitting local businesses and other area cultural, historic, and environmental attractions as well.

Done and proclaimed this 16ᵗʰ day of June 2014.

Robert F. Apgar, Mayor

Attest

Julie A. Hennessy, City Clerk - Auditor

The Stetson Kindred of America, Inc.
PO Box 31, Norwell, MA 02061
Established 1905

August 30, 2016

Mr. Michael Solari
Mr. J T Thompson
1031 Camphor Lane
DeLand, FL 32720

Dear Mr. Solari and Mr. Thompson:

The Officers, Directors and members take great pleasure in welcoming you as Honorary Members of the Stetson Kindred of America, Inc. You can take considerable satisfaction in knowing that you are the first Designees outside the Corporation to enjoy Honorary membership status since founding of the Kindred in 1905.

In response to a letter of commendation submitted to our Board of Directors last fall by Kindred member Beverly Colton-Cochrane, the Board voted to approve your candidacy for Honorary Membership. Honorary status was subsequently unanimously approved by the membership at our Annual Meeting on August 21, 2016.

Extraordinary contributions to perpetuation of the Stetson legacy and heritage are rare. It is an honor for us to recognize your steadfast devotion to the reclamation and architectural and historical restoration of the John B. Stetson house in DeLand, and to make enjoyment of the fruits of your labors available to the public for special events and historical education. It is truly a remarkable achievement.

Enclosed please find your official Honorary Membership Certificate, which is bestowed for life with all the rights and privileges as outlined in our Bylaws.

We hope that at some time in the not-too-distant future you can join us at one of our Annual Meeting weekends, which is always held the third weekend in August.

With deepest appreciation,

Linda Brooks

Linda Brooks, Membership Secretary
The Stetson Kindred of America, Inc.

Stetson

This Certifies That

J T Thompson
of DeLand, FL

has been elected an

Honorary Member of

The Stetson Kindred of America, Inc.

Dated at Norwell, Massachusetts

This 21st day of August 2016

Buede Brooks

Membership Secretary

Certificate of Recognition

Whereas, the Stetson Mansion Holiday Home Tour "The Magic of Christmas is Kindness" received first place in the USA Today's 10 Best Holiday Home Tour contest; and

Whereas, the Stetson Mansion was built in 1886 by famed hat maker and philanthropist John B. Stetson which served as his winter retreat and the Stetson Mansion was Florida's first luxury home and is regarded as one of America's top 300 historic homes, and;

Whereas, the mansion was the most modern home in Florida when it was built and Thomas Edison, a friend of Stetson, installed the electrical system which allowed for one of the first sets of electric Christmas tree lights to be used on a tree in the Stetson Mansion. The old tradition started by Stetson and Edison is still continued today by lighting the Christmas tree in the parlor with the same electric outlet that Edison installed for that very first string of tree lights; and

Whereas, the Holiday Home Tour featured 10 different designs, each inspired by different Christmas carols, and

Whereas, we extend our congratulations to J.T. Thompson and Michael Solari, the owners of the Stetson Mansion who have worked so hard to make the visitors' experience at Stetson Mansion memorable and our thanks for the business that their success has generated for others in our City.

Now, therefore, I, Robert F. Apgar, Mayor of the City of DeLand, and on behalf of the City Commission extend our congratulations to the Stetson Mansion, and its owners J.T. Thompson and Michael Solari for being recognized as USA Today's Best Holiday Home Tour and urge all our citizens to recognize the Stetson Mansion as a valuable historic resource. Further, we acknowledge the significance of this recognition for our community and the positive impact it will have on tourism in DeLand and West Volusia benefitting local businesses and other area cultural, historic, and environmental attractions as well.

Done and proclaimed this 22nd day of January 2019.

_____

Robert F. Apgar, Mayor

Attest

_____

Julie A. Hennessy, City Clerk - Auditor

STETSON MANSION

Copyright © October, 2014

By JT Thompson

All rights reserved. 2014

ISBN 13: 978-1-4675-9431-8

Printed By:
Dolphin Printing & Design, Inc.
4751 E. Moody Blvd. Suite 6E
Bunnell, FL 32110
dolphinprinting@bellsouth.net